SpringerBriefs in Computer Science

Series Editors
Stan Zdonik
Shashi Shekhar
Jonathan Katz
Xindong Wu
Lakhmi C. Jain
David Padua
Xuemin (Sherman) Shen
Borko Furht
V.S. Subrahmanian
Martial Hebert
Katsushi Ikeuchi
Bruno Siciliano
Sushil Jajodia
Newton Lee

AF793696

More information about this series at http://www.springer.com/series/10028

Elise Lemle • Katherine Bomkamp
Marcella Klein Williams • Elizabeth Cutbirth

Two Bit Circus and the Future of Entertainment

Springer

Elise Lemle
Two Bit Circus
Los Angeles, CA, USA

Katherine Bomkamp
Two Bit Circus
Los Angeles, CA, USA

Marcella Klein Williams
Solve for Pattern
Los Angeles, CA, USA

Elizabeth Cutbirth
Los Angeles, CA, USA

ISSN 2191-5768 ISSN 2191-5776 (electronic)
SpringerBriefs in Computer Science
ISBN 978-3-319-25791-4 ISBN 978-3-319-25793-8 (eBook)
DOI 10.1007/978-3-319-25793-8

Library of Congress Control Number: 2015959076

Springer Cham Heidelberg New York Dordrecht London
© The Author(s) 2015
This work is subject to copyright. All rights are reserved by the Publisher, whether the whole or part of the material is concerned, specifically the rights of translation, reprinting, reuse of illustrations, recitation, broadcasting, reproduction on microfilms or in any other physical way, and transmission or information storage and retrieval, electronic adaptation, computer software, or by similar or dissimilar methodology now known or hereafter developed.
The use of general descriptive names, registered names, trademarks, service marks, etc. in this publication does not imply, even in the absence of a specific statement, that such names are exempt from the relevant protective laws and regulations and therefore free for general use.
The publisher, the authors and the editors are safe to assume that the advice and information in this book are believed to be true and accurate at the date of publication. Neither the publisher nor the authors or the editors give a warranty, express or implied, with respect to the material contained herein or for any errors or omissions that may have been made.

Printed on acid-free paper

Springer International Publishing AG Switzerland is part of Springer Science+Business Media (www.springer.com)

Prologue

Abstract Educating a future STEM literate workforce requires a paradigm shift in how we approach teaching those disciplines. Collaboration with technological innovators can bring experiential learning opportunities to the classroom. Exposing students to these innovators and their work can enable those students to see their own pathways to STEM careers.

Prologue

I adjust the straps to my head, carefully, to keep them from snagging my hair. I already feel woefully out of place, but this young guy is nice. It'll be okay. I'm standing in the shop of Two Bit Circus where Hector Alvarez, the Creative Director, helps me try out the virtual reality headset. My eyes adjust to the scene. The impact of the immersive experience is just so much more "wow" than I anticipated. Let's be honest, this isn't my world, and my expectations hadn't been stretched enough to be ready for it. I'm a little scared, and my hand squirms around until I find Hector's shoulder. There's something reassuring about simple human connectedness. My fear subsides, and I am in another world and awed by the strange mix of both virtual and reality. The experience opens a window for me into the world of technology, the innovators that create it, and the pathways that led them there.

Introduction

I'm an educator. Our profession prepares children for the future, yet classrooms today look astonishingly similar to those of decades past. Meanwhile the rest of our life, from work to play, has galloped along in an incredible era of innovation. Transforming classrooms to meet the future requires more than the spark of a great idea. It's some mix of the right team, the right idea, and the right time.

Fig. 1 Popular Mechanic's 2014 Breakthrough awardees, Brent Bushnell and Eric Gradman of Two Bit Circus

Science, math, and engineering are disciplines children have struggled with mightily in this country for nearly a generation. Brent Bushnell, CEO of Two Bit Circus, summarizes his plan for overhauling how we teach children these essential subjects in three words: "lasers, fire, and robots." Two Bit Circus won Popular Mechanics Magazine's 2014 Breakthrough Award. Their achievement is making children want to learn (Howard 2014). Two Bit Circus offers an instructive model bridging the world of emerging technology with learning. Overhauling how we teach means rolling up our sleeves and diving into a system where words like "lasers, fire, and robots" can evoke fear among faint-of-heart school leaders. This is a story of how bravery, camaraderie, and sheer fun combine in a quest to help learners design their own better world.

It Began with a Rube Goldberg Machine

When they were part of a team constructing a 40,000 square foot Rube Goldberg machine, the last adjective Brent Bushnell and Eric Gradman would have used to describe their work was educational. A Rube Goldman machine is an elaborate piece of engineering that performs a very basic task. The one Bushnell and Gradman worked on was the centerpiece of a music video for the band OK Go. The commercial and critical success of that Rube Goldberg machine provided the initial spark that would ultimately lead to a dedicated program designed to reignite students' interest in technological careers and inspire the next generation of inventors (Two Bit Circus 2014).

The pair went on to found Two Bit Circus, an engineering entertainment company that is reinventing the ways that people of all ages play and learn. Their unique productions encourage playful collaboration across multiple platforms in interactive and meaningful ways. After successfully installing games and interactive experiences at amusement parks, restaurants, and corporate events, they decided to design their own STEM event (Two Bit Circus 2014).

While exploring the potential of such an event, Bushnell, Gradman, and the Two Bit Circus team became aware of heartbreaking statistics describing the decline of student proficiency and interest in valuable STEM disciplines: science, technology, engineering, and math. However, they saw a real opportunity to reengage students by including art—transforming STEM into STEAM and inspiring a new pathway for learning (Two Bit Circus 2014).

That was the genesis of STEAM Carnival—an entertainment showcase packed with lasers, fire, and robots. The event leverages children's interests in music, fashion, and games to expose them to STEAM and get them excited to create.

Fig. 2 Children playing with interactive musical chairs during the Los Angeles STEAM Carnival

Fig. 3 Kids experimenting with an interactive musical art installation at the Los Angeles STEAM Carnival

Portfolio of Experiential Learning

Each Two Bit Circus project incorporates one or more of the named seven experiential learning characteristics: locus of control, physical involvement, intellectual involvement, social and emotional involvement, context, element of risk, and embedded reflection (McLain 2014). These physical and digital playgrounds engineer purposeful play, the recipe for high-quality learning designed to drive both content mastery and constructive understanding.

This bias toward experiential learning reflects changing landscapes. Our business leaders and economic forecasters implore education to keep up for the health and continued prosperity of our nation.

Educators can no longer afford to go it alone. The days of replicating decades-old practices are gone. Today we are building while we go. Doing that successfully requires collaboration with innovators who are brave enough to try new approaches.

We hope to instill in school children the twenty-first-century competencies of communication, collaboration, creativity, and critical thinking (National Education Association 2012). Those same competencies are going to help us construct the future of education. Two Bit Circus is just one example of private sector collaboration in STEM Education. Theirs is the story of a collaboration that hits at the right time, has the right ideas, and is composed of the right team.

The Right Team

"A band of nerds," that's how Brent Bushnell refers to the Two Bit Circus team. This creative group has talents well outside the typical bounds of science, technology, and engineering. Their path to the Big Top included interesting stops along the way such as winner of North American Unicycling Championship, professional whistler, singer, actor, educator, artist, and more. The diversity of backgrounds, talents, passions, and perspectives makes for lively collaboration that is harnessed into work that is actually useful.

The work done in their shop is largely based on emerging technology with innovative twists on old ideas. It is both exhilarating and sometimes scary. Prototyping, testing, tweaking, and iterating happen every day. Two Bit Circus' "office" is a working shop toward the back with couches and desks in the front. Electronic widgets are everywhere. This band is a happy lot, and it's likely that their humor and easiness grease the skids for the tough collaborative work in that it takes to integrate slivers of genius to create something great. According to Brent Bushnell: "What we

Fig. 4 The Two Bit Circus "band of nerds"

do is fun. The people here are charting new ways of communicating, learning, working and playing…and we make our living doing this STEAM thing. We make a good living doing this STEAM thing. We're creating things and doing things first—hard things! But what we're proving is that these ideas have a reality. They are real, and what we're showing with our work is the physical manifestation of that to inspire more people to make this **their** reality" (2014).

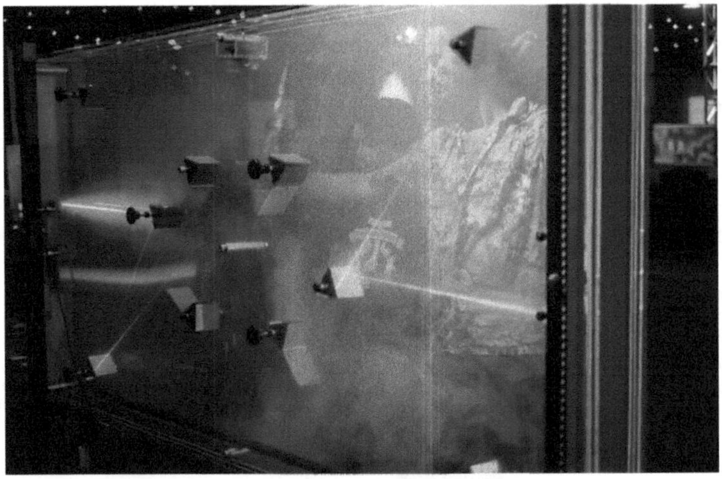

Fig. 5 Two Bit Circus team member adjusts mirrors during a test of a "Laser Foosball" game

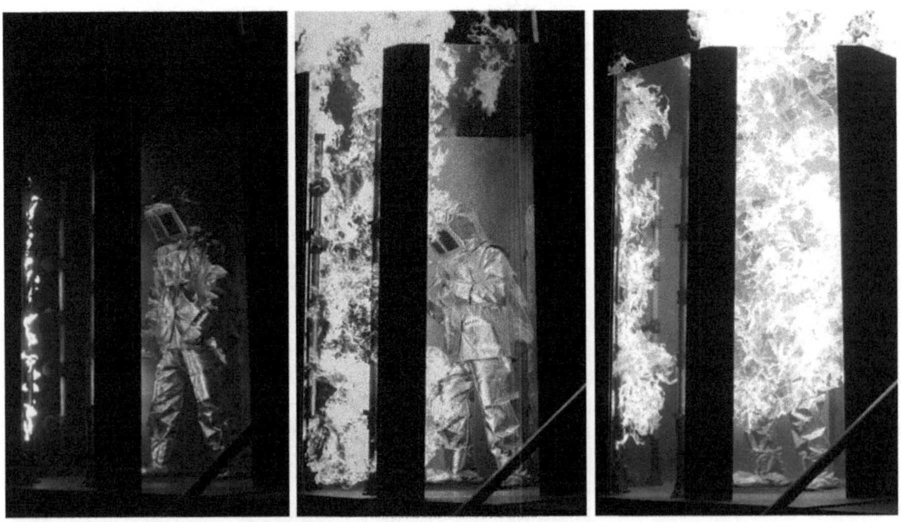

Fig. 6 Time lapse imagery detailing "Dunk Tank Flambé" at the Los Angeles STEAM Carnival

Bumping Against Reality

A signature production of Two Bit Circus is STEAM Carnival. It is a modern take on the traveling circus, bridging high-tech amusement with project-based learning to inspire students of all ages to pursue science, technology, engineering, art, and math. The goal is to activate curiosity in young explorers through hands-on project, mentorship, workshops, and dynamic physical interaction with high-tech games (Two Bit Circus 2014).

Ideas, projects, and products like the STEAM Carnival are trotted out when they are still young so they can "bump against reality."

That is how innovation moves forward.

In preparation for STEAM Carnival, the Two Bit Circus Learning Team piloted their particular perspective in STEAM on a hot summer day in a school cafeteria. Trays with unfamiliar controllers were arranged next to bananas, paper clips, and foil for hands-on inquiry surrounding the secrets of conductivity. Any educator could imagine where that lesson might run off the rails; school Superintendent Colleen Robertson gave it a go anyways, partnering with a crowd of self-described "carnies."

The spirit of innovation took educators somewhere they might not otherwise have gone. Succeeding or failing as an educator is always done with an audience. Safety is found in tradition, and it takes courage to break from the tried and true. People with guts do it—and they do it again. They do not just talk about it. They do not wait for someone else to work out all the kinks. Fear of getting it wrong plays second fiddle to the desire to get it right.

Fig. 7 Members of the Two Bit Circus Learning Team working with students during a curriculum pilot

Joining the Circus

The group of inventors, developers, and performers that make up Two Bit Circus is representative of who we need in order to make our future. Characters like that are generally hard to track down. Authors, illustrators, and artists have traditional ways of signing their work. Credits trailing a movie point to the people who contributed to the production and inform the audience of each contributor's specific role. That is not the case for the highly collaborative work made possible by engineers, industrial designers, fabricators, and more. Asking the public to name the roles and titles of today's innovators would prove disappointing.

The result is that today's youth lack role models in technology and innovation. It is difficult for them to picture themselves in STEM careers without seeing who these people are and what they do. Connecting people with ideas and products helps demystify the process of developing something new and useful. Shifting the next generation from being consumers of technology to inventors of it requires an understanding that today's advancements do not just drop from on high. They need to see that there is an ensemble of people working behind the scenes bringing simply every single innovation to us.

Allowing children a glimpse of the people behind the work changes minds and even career trajectories. I stood in front of a classroom of eighth grade students as Two Bit Circus came to them through an online conference. Before the event went live, I asked for a show of hands of who was interested in pursuing a STEAM career. A couple nervous hands inched up. Katherine Bomkamp and Elise Lemle from Two Bit Circus connected in for a 30-min conversation about the shop, the work taking place there, and a bouncy tour showing off the people, the tools, the products, and the workspaces, nothing fancy—just simple and personable. What came across was that the people doing this work were accessible and approachable. They were happy to talk to the children and share their interesting paths. Their passion did not have to be explained. It was obvious. We said our goodbyes.

The connection clicked off. I again asked students who was interested in a STEAM career. This time hands across the room shot up.

Connecting the students in the classroom with the innovators at Two Bit Circus enabled those children to see behind the magic. Technology was no longer just a product one buys at a store. It was now something made by people, and those students could see who those people were and could imagine themselves pursuing the same career.

Connecting to the person allows us to see behind the magic and reminds us that not only do we enjoy the world created, but we can also emulate the designer and create our own world. Like Hector offering a shoulder for me to ground myself, it is this simple human connectedness that echoes "me too, come with me, I'll show you."

Fig. 8 Two Bit Circus "carnies" in logo jumpsuits during filming of the 2013 STEAM Carnival Kickstarter campaign video

Conclusion

As an educator charged with inspiring the next generation, I need to connect students with innovators and the technology they create. Those connections will give children the materials they need to paint a picture of their future selves in STEAM-related careers. Only through collaboration between educators and innovators, like the carnies at Two Bit Circus, can we give students the experiences they need to inspire them to excel in STEAM disciplines.

Solve for Pattern
Los Angeles, CA, USA

Marcella Klein Williams

References

Bushnell B (2014) Welcoming remarks. In: STEAM Gala, Two Bit Circus, Los Angeles, 22 Oct 2014

Howard D (2014) Think science is boring? These gentlemen would like a word with you. In: Popular Mechanics. http://www.popularmechanics.com/technology/design/a12809/science-and-math-are-not-boring-breakthrough-awards-2014/. Accessed 29 June 2015

McLain B (2014) ELVIS: Experiential Learning Variables and Indicators Scale. http://www.xsci.org/research-2/experiential-learning-theory/#!prettyPhoto[topbox1]/0/. Accessed 29 June 2015

National Education Association (2012) Preparing 21st century students for a global society: an educator's guide to the "Four C's". http://www.nea.org/assets/docs/A-Guide-to-Four-Cs.pdf. Accessed 29 June 2015

Two Bit Circus (2014) Unpublished manuscript

Contents

1 Swinging from Digital Playgrounds 1
1 Introduction: Computer Revolution 1
2 Technology Changes Everything 2
3 Shifting from Consumers to Creators 3
4 The Two Bit Circus Approach to Purposeful Play 3
5 Conclusion 7
References 7

2 At the Intersection of Digital and Physical Play: The Lifecycle of a Two Bit Circus Game 9
1 Introduction 9
2 A Passion for Play 9
3 The Two Bit Circus Game 10
4 The Process 12
5 Buttonwall: A Case Study 13
6 Conclusion 16
References 16

3 Story Room: The Computer as Live-Action Storyteller for Adaptive Game Play 17
1 Sixty Minutes to Escape 17
2 Digital Puzzles 18
3 Theatrical Shifts 18
4 The Third Space 19
5 History 20
6 High-Tech Gameplay 22
7 Moving Forward 23
8 Conclusion 23
References 24

4 Virtual Reality and the Future of Entertainment 25
1 Prologue 25
2 Definitions 25
3 Early Innovation 26
4 Current Platforms 27
4.1 The Three-Dimensional Puzzle 29
4.2 Creative Decision-Making: Technology and Content 30
4.3 Mediums and Narrative Opportunities 31
4.4 VR Innovation @ Two Bit Circus 31
4.5 Facing New Challenges 35
5 Conclusion: Envisioning the Future 36
References 36

5 Interview with Brent N. Bushnell, Co-Founder and CEO of Two Bit Circus 39
1 Interview with Brent N. Bushnell 39

Chapter 1
Swinging from Digital Playgrounds

Abstract The world is in the middle of a technological revolution, with computers and technology integrated into every aspect of modern life. We see the implications of this in the workforce, with jobs in STEM (science, technology, engineering, math) fields accounting for more than 10 % of jobs in the US, a number that is constantly on the rise (http://www.forbes.com/sites/kathryndill/2014/07/03/the-top-paying-stem-jobs-for-recent-grads/). Paradigms are shifting in the classroom to prepare our students for this new twenty-first century workforce with educators, administrators, and parents alike embracing technology as a way to enhance the educational environment. Two Bit Circus looks to support this consumer to creator mindset, offering curriculum, workshops, and professional learning focused on incorporating the creative design process into engineering as seen through the process of game making.

1 Introduction: Computer Revolution

There is no denying we are in the midst of a technological revolution. Computers used to fill entire rooms and unless you worked for IBM or went to Stanford, chances are you would never have the opportunity to see a computer, much less use one daily. We have come a long way in the past 10 years with regards to computers and technological innovation. In 2013, 83.8 % of all American households had a computer with 78.5 % of all households reporting internet usage (File and Ryan 2014).

Children's computer usage provides compelling evidence of the computer revolution. According to research done by Rasmussen College, 90 % of children have used a computer by age two. Recent data shows that by age three, most children prefer digital toys to non-digital toys and by age five, 50 % of children are using tablets and tablet devices on a regular basis. By age seven, more than 60 % of children are playing console and handheld video games (Column Five Media 2013).

Modern games live at the crossroads of children and their technology usage, evidence of the perfect marriage of a child's high literacy in tech and a love of explorative play. Since video games were first introduced for at-home use in the 1970s, children have come to view computers very differently than their parents. This is due in part to Nolan Bushnell (father of Two Bit Circus CEO Brent Bushnell), founder of Atari and the popular restaurant chain Chuck E. Cheese. While many

© The Author(s) 2015
E. Lemle et al., *Two Bit Circus and the Future of Entertainment*,
SpringerBriefs in Computer Science, DOI 10.1007/978-3-319-25793-8_1

adults were first exposed to computers as a tool for business and industry, usually reserved for the wealthy or the corporate consumer, from an early age contemporary children embrace technology for connectivity, social interaction, and most importantly, for learning and play.

Video games have emerged as an art form, immersive media, and marketing platform, as well as a serious contender in the commercial marketplace. In 2013, sales of video games generated $21 billion dollars for the United States economy (Cox 2014). Twenty-nine percent of all video game users in the United States are under the age of 18 and the average US household owns at least one dedicated game console, PC, or smartphone. Gaming is also becoming more of a family affair, with 91 % of parents whose children play video games present when the game is purchased or played (Entertainment Software Association 2014). Sixty-eight percent of parents whose children play video games believe that game play provides mental stimulation or educational benefit.

We are in the midst of a technological revolution, made apparent by our technologically-literate children. Computers are redefining the way people interact with each other, learn about the world around them, and, changing our definitions of what is considered fun.

2 Technology Changes Everything

Today's children are the first generation of "digital natives", individuals surrounded by advanced technology (Prensky 2001). From the time they wake up to the time they go to sleep, children consume technology at home and at school, spending as much time on the digital playground as they are on the physical playground. As a result, contemporary children learn and process information differently than previous generations. The education system in America is struggling to keep up. Educators who grew up in the pre-digital age, or "digital immigrants" as coined by Marc Prensky, struggle to reach a population that essentially speaks a different language, and has a radically different view of a more interconnected and accessible world (2001).

Technology is increasingly integrated into the twenty-first century workforce as well as in the classroom. Schools are making a conscious effort to keep up with technological advancements, incorporating tech into teaching practices and in the physical classrooms to enhance the learning experience for both students and educators. Walking into a classroom today, you may find a class of fifth graders researching on iPads or second graders learning about weather using online maps. Increasing numbers schools are providing students with laptops to use daily in class. More classrooms are utilizing flat screen TVs, digital whiteboards, high speed wireless internet, high resolution projectors, and sophisticated classroom management software.

Technological advances are shifting classroom pedagogy, especially as it applies to content delivery. Concepts such as the "flipped classroom" provide educators the opportunity to spend their classroom time working together to solve problems and answer questions as students access video lectures online at home (Edutopia 2015). According to a report by CompTIA, titled *Opportunities in the Education Market*, 78 % of K-12 educators and administrators believe that technology has positively impacted their classrooms and the productivity of students (Lytle 2011).

The computer revolution has brought about undeniable changes in the way we live, work, communicate, and learn. This culture and paradigm shift is most evident in the children who are growing up in this generation. Two Bit Circus recognizes this opportunity. By leveraging children's interests and technological proficiency to encourage learning and to develop critical thinking skills, Two Bit Circus is preparing learners with skills needed to be successful in the twenty-first century workforce. Two Bit Circus refers to this change as the consumer-to-creator shift.

3 Shifting from Consumers to Creators

Researchers at elite academic institutions, famed psychologists, and hosts of popular morning talk shows like to weigh in on the impact that technology has on how children grow and learn. One thing is clear: children today are passive consumers of technology. Hand an 8-year-old an iPhone and chances are, he can turn it on and beat your high score on Angry Birds. However, ask him about the computing power of the phone, the software running on the phone, or the programming languages used to write Angry Birds, and you will likely get a blank stare in response. Modern society faces the challenge of shifting children from passive consumers of technology to critically thinking technologists. If we want children to be able to understand the technology they use everyday, then we need to start providing them with the tools to understand them from an early age (Stepner 2015).

Two Bit Circus is addressing this challenge and inspiring the next generation of inventors. Children love games. As game making is Two Bit Circus' core competency, fusing learning and the design process with games is a natural fit for the company. Children come from a place of authority when they are playing games, and meeting them on this level has proven very successful in keeping children engaged and interested in learning new content.

4 The Two Bit Circus Approach to Purposeful Play

Brent Bushnell and Eric Gradman helped to redefine engineering as a discipline when they were part of a team that built a giant Rube Goldberg machine which was featured in a music video for the band OK Go. As the video went viral, Bushnell and Gradman found themselves being contacted frequently by an unexpected new fan base, teachers. They were approached by educators across the country asking about hands-on and project based ways to introduce engineering to their students, which also explored engineering concepts that would prepare their students for success.

Bushnell and Gradman realized that while the work of Two Bit Circus was grounded in entertainment, the games and attractions built by the company also had deep learning components that could be used to inspire the next generation of inventors, developers, performers, and engineers. The company's large scale, multiplayer games showcase inventive concepts, and Bushnell and Gradman are frequently quoted saying they want to make science and engineering "the new rock and roll" (Littlejohn 2014). The company has become evangelists of STEAM, an acronym standing for science, technology, engineering, art, and math. A twist on the commonly used STEM acronym, Two Bit Circus incorporates the artistic design process into engineering, exposing the creativity used in the design of each product (Fig. 1.1).

Given Two Bit Circus' expertise in game development, it is natural for the company to encourage the educational shift towards STEAM through the process of inventing games. Game making is an expansive topic, with countless textbooks written about the types of games, game theory, game logic, video game design, never mind the actual art of designing a fun, playable game. Game creation also requires a suite of learned skills including programming, physical fabrication, and

Fig. 1.1 Two Bit Circus game creation session at BritWeek's 2015 "Coding for Kids" event (Reproduced from Gelert 2015)

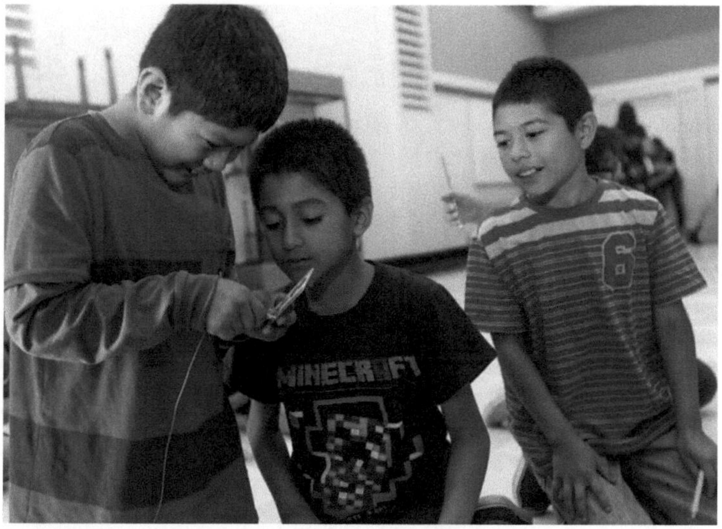

Fig. 1.2 Third-graders explore the MaKey MaKey video game controller during a Two Bit Circus workshop

knowledge of electronics. Given these challenges, engaging a room full of young children in a technical activity could seem like a daunting task.

However, learning new skills need not be intimidating and can prove to be greatly enjoyable. By taking a project-based approach to promote active exploration, STEAM-based curriculum ignites an active shift from consumer to creator (Fig. 1.2).

One popular example of a product promoting the consumer to creator shift is the MaKey MaKey, an Arduino-based microcontroller developed by MIT Media Lab's Jay Silver and Eric Rosenbaum is (Joylabz 2015). With the MaKey MaKey, children use unconventional materials, such as bananas, grapes, tinfoil, and Play Doh, to explore conductivity and microcontrollers, ultimately creating their own video game controllers.

Recognizing an opportunity for impact, educators and content providers are actively developing learning content to further explore curricular connections between the MaKey MaKey and STEAM. For example, Two Bit Circus' MaKeyCade curriculum guides students through the process of creating their own digital and physical games through exercises which build basic programming skills and command logic. Through a series of lessons, students build on their programming skills to incorporate the MaKey MaKey microcontroller, and later build physical game pieces out of recycled materials for enhanced integration that emphasizes every step of the engineering design process.

Fig. 1.3 Educators participating in Two Bit Circus Professional Learning session in wearable technology

While Two Bit Circus remains committed to working with students, the company recognizes that educators play an essential role in inspiring the next generation of inventors. Two Bit Circus is teaching and providing STEAM professional learning workshops for educators and industry professionals that explore approaches to STEAM content and pedagogy, the engineering design process, and the learning opportunities inherent in game making (Fig. 1.3).

Two Bit Circus' version of the engineering design process (Fig. 1.4), consisting of inspiration, explore, plan, make, share and revise, is a major focus for the professional learning sessions as the iterative design process permeates every aspect of research and development work at the company. Current curricular offerings in the professional learning series include "Game Making for Educators", a top level view of the design process as applied to game making, and participants rapid prototype games using basic off the shelf items. Additional offering MaKeyCade incorporates programming, basic electronics, and physical fabrication to get participants thinking in the mindset of a game designer. A wearable electronics workshop gets learners designing a patch or other wearable piece that incorporates design elements with electronics sewn to the fabric with conductive thread. Theory-based sessions include "STEAM 101" where learners examine STEAM as an emerging educational concept, exploring ways to implement STEAM into their classrooms or professional practice, and "Creativity and Engagement", which examines creativity as a learned skill to craft and hone, a departure from traditional thought that creativity is possessed from birth.

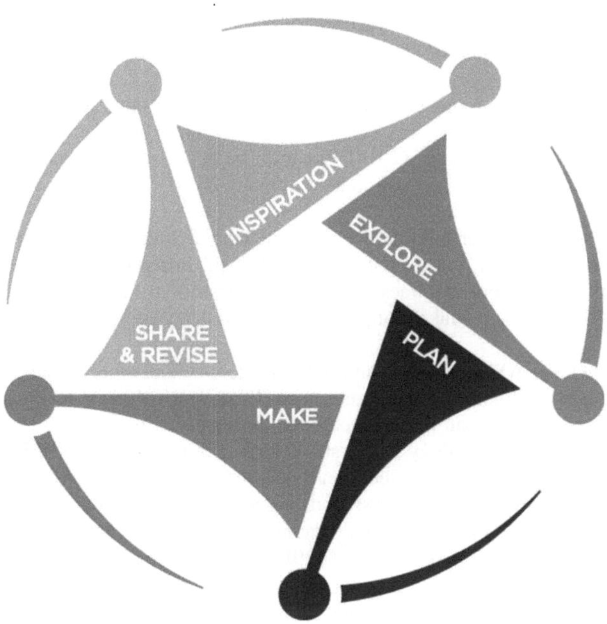

Fig. 1.4 Design process diagram

5 Conclusion

Two Bit Circus is blurring the lines between digital and physical play. By infusing the engineering design process with a spirit of invention and creativity, children will actively shift from consumers of technology to creators of technology. The educational landscape is starting to reflect this new thought leadership, with game based learning and technology being more consciously incorporated into the classrooms with varying levels of integration and success.

The company is exploring multiple avenues to promote and support this new educational paradigm; writing curriculum for STEAM-focused learning and offering professional learning sessions for educators and industry professionals. These programs seek to actively shift students and educators from consumers to creators and inspire the next generation of inventors.

References

Column Five Media (2013) Infographic: technology development stages for kids. In: Rasmussen College School of Education Blog. http://www.rasmussen.edu/degrees/education/blog/infographic-technology-development-stages-for-children/. Accessed 16 Apr 2015

Cox K (2014) It's time to start treating the video game industry like the $21 billion business it is. In: Consumerist. http://consumerist.com/2014/06/09/its-time-to-start-treating-video-game-industry-like-the-21-billion-business-it-is/. Accessed 9 June 2015

Dill K (2014) The top paying STEM jobs for recent grads. In: Forbes Magazine. http://www.forbes.com/sites/kathryndill/2014/07/03/the-top-paying-stem-jobs-for-recent-grads/. Accessed 22 June 2015

Edutopia (2015) Flipped Classroom. http://www.edutopia.org/blogs/tag/flipped-classroom Accessed 1 July 2015

Entertainment Software Association (2014) Essential facts about the computer and video game industry. http://www.theesa.com/wp-content/uploads/2014/10/ESA_EF_2014.pdf. Accessed 11 June 2015

File T, Ryan C (2014) Computer and internet use in the United States: 2013. American Community Survey Reports. Available via the US Census Bureau. http://www.census.gov/content/dam/Census/library/publications/2014/acs/acs-28.pdf. Accessed 16 Apr 2015

Joylabz (2015) About Makey Makey. http://www.makeymakey.com/about.php. Accessed 1 July 2015

Littlejohn D (2014) STEAM Carnival bringing lasers, robots, and more to San Pedro in October. In: Daily Breeze. http://www.dailybreeze.com/lifestyle/20140921/steam-carnival-bringing-lasers-robots-and-more-to-san-pedro-in-october. Accessed 25 June 2015

Lytle R (2011) Emerging technology has positive impact in classroom. In: US News and World Report. http://www.usnews.com/education/high-schools/articles/2011/07/14/study-emerging-technology-has-positive-impact-in-classroom. Accessed 22 June 2015

Prensky M (2001) Digital natives, digital immigrants. http://www.marcprensky.com/writing/Prensky%20-%20Digital%20Natives,%20Digital%20Immigrants%20-%20Part1.pdf. Accessed 20 May 2015

Stepner D (2015) Why the future will be made by creators, not consumers. In: Wired. http://www.wired.com/2014/12/future-made-by-creators-not-consumers/. Accessed 4 June 2015

Chapter 2
At the Intersection of Digital and Physical Play: The Lifecycle of a Two Bit Circus Game

Abstract What are the connection points between the digital and physical worlds? With the rise of the Internet of Things (IoT) and ever-immersive gameplay, we are increasingly bridging the perceptible world of everyday items with the intangible possibilities of the digital realm. This chapter explores the intersection of the physical and digital realms through the design and creation of Two Bit Circus' novel games.

1 Introduction

It's 5 pm on a Thursday. A self-described "big band of nerds" sinks deep into dilapidated sofas, attempting not to tip the beers balancing on their open laptops.

It's brainstorm time.

Ideas are spit out in rapid fire: ranging from the absurd, to the derivative, to kernels of brilliance, half-baked concepts fly and are quickly processed and recorded. The group remains supportive despite the range of implausible to executable ideas. Metaphorically, the team is reveling in what Walt Disney would refer to as his "blue skies room": the space where all ideas are possible and all opportunities considered (Glei and Belsky 2011).

An hour or two of fierce concentration punctuated with gleeful shouts and several ideas emerge. As the carnies finish their drinks, an enthusiastic smaller team assembles to begin planning the next prototype.

This event is the first step in the lifecycle of the Two Bit Circus game.

2 A Passion for Play

While only a few of the Two Bit Circus "carnies" have formal education in game design—it is a group that has been immersed in the form, for some since birth. The son of the creator of Atari and Chuck E. Cheese, CEO and Roustabout Brent Bushnell recalls spending hours programming a single dot to move back and forth across a screen (Personal conversation 2014). Other team members spend their weekends immersed in the latest Steam titles or crafting innovative lawn games.

© The Author(s) 2015

E. Lemle et al., *Two Bit Circus and the Future of Entertainment*,
SpringerBriefs in Computer Science, DOI 10.1007/978-3-319-25793-8_2

This enthusiasm and passion for games radiates throughout the Big Top (the nickname for the company's downtown Los Angeles workshop): large prototyping monitors will be surreptitiously co-opted for an afternoon X-Box-fueled dance party. A tetherball tied to an otherwise scrap piece of pipe in the back of the shop, hours spent discussing the latest immersive adventure games.

Every fortnight, the Big Top hosts a game night for carnies and game design friends. This event serves as an opportunity for carnies and others to test out new games and evaluate existing commercial games in a playful and supportive environment. Through this process, the team has become adept at both identifying important qualities of entertaining and effective games.

3 The Two Bit Circus Game

While there are no summative traits that characterize every Two Bit Circus game, Two Bit Circus games can be generally identified by the integration of physical and digital elements and a deliberate emphasis on social play.

Integration of the physical and digital elements is paramount; the technology behind the games is often at the core of game play. Hardware is often the single most important piece of a Two Bit Circus game. To that end, the build process typically begins with an exploration of the hardware needed to execute the project. The development team considers what "guts" will yield the most effective and engaging platform for the refined concept (Cutbirth 2015). Commonly used hardware includes Raspberry Pis, Arduinos, Teensies, and Mac Minis. The limitation of the hardware plays an integral role in the refinement and iterative design even at such an early stage.

Unlike arcarde cabinets found in the mall arcades of the eighties, Two Bit Circus games are explicitly multiplayer, encouraging players to physically engage with one another in playful competition. In practice, this social, physical play ranges from giant trackballs controlling projected bubbles (Fig. 2.1) to life size, accelerometer-equipped rocking horses driving onscreen avatars (Figs. 2.2 and 2.3).

Fig. 2.1 Two Bit Circus' Hexaball, a game comprised of giant trackballs controlling a projected image

Fig. 2.2 Patrons at Two Bit Circus' 2014 Los Angeles STEAM Carnival enjoying a high-tech game

Fig. 2.3 Engineers calibrating Two Bit Circus' "Laser Maze"

The games are often rough around the edges, sometimes with visible signs of strain and wear. Typically constructed out of wood, the games feature classic arcade buttons, and various found materials. While not ideal for long-term use, there is a certain charm to the unfinished nature of the games. The prototype aesthetic is accessible and inspiring, as if the player might, with a few tools, a computer, and some elbow grease, construct his or her own weekend version.

Two Bit Circus games have very few rules. So few rules in fact, it is occasionally difficult for the timid player to figure out how to play the game. The open-ended nature of the games allows for players to create new ways of engaging with the content, often beyond the creators' intent. Re-play ability is a crucial component for success. The team strives for Bushnell's "easy to play, impossible to master" idiom when creating and testing games.

4 The Process

After an initial brainstorm, the team divides into a small crew that is responsible for the first build. This smaller team distills the larger ideas into an executable project and delegates a first round of build tasks. Preliminary code is typically prototyped during this development stage, which, once up and running, is paired with jump wires and breadboards, which are eventually replaced with buttons, circuit boards, and solder. As Two Bit Circus games integrate both hardware and software, it is extremely important that functional components are introduced at an early stage.

After the development team has vetted the initial concept, the exterior or enclosure begins to take shape. Once the initial enclosure has been designed, the team decides on the placement of peripherals (buttons, lights, etc.). While a seemingly straightforward task, this small step is of crucial importance; the team must consider aesthetics, gameplay, fairness, safety, and ergonomics (Cutbirth 2015). Oftentimes, the enclosure is adjusted to accommodate for peripheral placement.

The team selects materials and rapidly prototypes a custom enclosure. At this stage in the process, the team also considers the primary venue in which the game will be played and how it will impact material options and choices (Cutbirth 2015). Typically cut on the Big Top laser cutters, most first enclosure prototypes consist of crude plywood construction held together with glue. The electronics are then installed in the enclosure and wired together.

After the first prototype is built, initial play testing begins. An extremely important part of the game design process, the initial test is typically conducted in-house. The core team will rally Two Bit Circus carnies from across the Big Top to play the game and provide feedback. As a result of this quick process, engineers will dig back into the code, identify bugs, and improve game play.

After the first round of playtests, the team will take some time polish the game (Cutbirth 2015). This includes cabling of internal wires, physical reinforcements, and external finish and decoration. For first versions, this process is typically done at the Big Top. Additional rounds of play testing, enclosure revisions, and software upgrades typically ensue.

Completed games go on the road, entertaining thousands at events across the country. In addition to the consistent revenue stream, events provide a valuable opportunity for additional user testing on a grand scale.

This exposure typically leads to another design cycle, after returning to the shop, the games are reevaluated and reworked. While the team may not go back through the full cycle for each improvement, this iterative process can take years.

Despite best efforts, this process does not always yield enjoyable or even playable games. As a side effect of the iterative design process, occasionally unwanted prototypes are stripped for parts and the shells unceremoniously left by the dumpster to bake in the Los Angeles sun. Other models they are left outside in the robot graveyard—evidence of past prototypes, which serve as reminders of the design process during Big Top tours.

While this process appears relatively linear, the development of a Two Bit Circus game remains cyclical and expansive.

5 Buttonwall: A Case Study

One of the team's earliest and most enduring games, Buttonwall, embodies the success and challenges of the team's approach to game development. The game is so core to the Two Bit Circus mythology that in 2015, when Two Bit Circus' Strategic Storyteller, Elizabeth Cutbirth, began a documentation project Buttonwall was the first game to be studied and profiled. Cutbirth's interviews with the games' original creators provide insight into the often non-linear path in the pursuit of multiplayer fun.

Brent Bushnell will often refer to the Buttonwall as a mash up of Wack-a-Mole and Twister. While the form factor has changed dramatically over time, at its core the game is a large box with a predetermined number of large arcade pushbuttons. Pairs of buttons illuminate at random and players must strike both illuminated buttons to score points. As players' score increases, three or more buttons will illuminate. As all buttons must be pushed simultaneously in order to score, players must get creative, often using elbows, knees, and even their heads to amass more points than their opponent. Players who remove the backside notice hundreds of wires all connected to a Raspberry Pi, a single board computer.

Bushnell and CTO and Mad Inventor, Eric Gradman built the first Buttonwall in 2008. As there were no actual buttons involved, the game began more as an interactive art piece, a four-by-four grid of multiple LEDs (Cutbirth 2015).

As the team began to focus more explicitly on multiplayer gameplay, the concept further developed to feature large arcade LED pushbuttons that could illuminate or turn off with a simple touch. This version was installed for an interactive play experience for Grand Mound in Washington. This version of the Buttonwall was actually a series of walls with large arcade style buttons in multiple colors (Fig. 2.4). While patrons greatly enjoyed the game play, the walls were plagued by physical and electrical problems that caused the games to break (Cutbirth 2015).

Fig. 2.4 An early Buttonwall prototype

The next version was optimized for two-player gameplay. For this version, the colors were simplified as players attempted to recreate different combinations on a large scale. While the game play and reliability improved with this iteration, the physical durability suffered (Cutbirth 2015).

As if to overcorrect for the flawed design, the next Buttonwall design resulted in an attractive physical interpretation of one of the company's logo elements, the gear. Created in anticipation of the company's 2013 Kickstarter campaign, this version of the game featured two giant enmeshed gears to house the opposing teams' buttons.

The resulting form factor visually enticing (Fig. 2.5), the game was incredibly fun to play as well as to observe. Players would hit illuminated buttons at rapid speeds while trying to spin their opponent's gear to knock off their flow.

However, during testing it became apparent that the game was unsafe. While players greatly enjoyed the game, the physical components were utilized in unexpected and potentially dangerous ways. Additionally, according to Gradman, this version was "difficult to service" (Cutbirth 2015). The game connected via wireless internet; despite best intentions, the creators agree that this version of the game "'was a mess'" (Cutbirth 2015). As if the described challenges did not provide reason enough for a new iteration, Gradman reported that "one of [the Buttonwalls] actually caught fire'" (Cutbirth 2015).

The next version returned to a rectangular wooden box suspended between two large pieces of truss (Fig. 2.6). As homage to the previous version, the bi-colored

Fig. 2.5 User testing of the "geared" Buttonwall

Fig. 2.6 A 2014 prototype of Buttonwall; this version evoked the previous geared version with overlapping buttons

buttons were arranged to overlap, requiring individual players to invade their opponents "zone" in order to score points. Players' scores and a 30-s countdown clock were displayed on multiple eight-segment displays. While the new form factor solved many of the challenges of the previous version, the software was seriously lacking and the resulting gameplay suffered (Cutbirth 2015).

Built into a hard-sided road case in 2014, the current version of Buttonwall is the most rugged and durable version to date. The software was completely rebuilt to complement the fresh exterior. However, as Bushnell relates, the software could be improved and the overall game would benefit from additional gameplay options (Cutbirth 2015). Although the current version solves some of the challenges associated with constant travel and use, the road case means it is still too heavy and unwieldy.

One of the greatest challenge with the Buttonwall development stems from the feeling that the "iterations have not been monotonic…[and not] every iteration has been a step forward…the learnings from past iterations have been forgotten…[and have not] always been applied to the current iterations" (Cutbirth 2015).

6 Conclusion

Two Bit Circus creates games that merge physical and digital play. The development of the Buttonwall provides insight into the Two Bit Circus' design process and how the company creates engaging experiences. As evidenced by the multiple design iterations from ideation to completion, the nonlinear creation process supports continual innovation.

References

Cutbirth E (2015) Key findings. Unpublished manuscript

Glei J, Belsky S (2011) Brainstorming 2.0: making ideas that really happen. http://99u.com/articles/6993/brainstorming-20-making-ideas-that-really-happen. Accessed 15 June 2015

Chapter 3
Story Room: The Computer as Live-Action Storyteller for Adaptive Game Play

Abstract What is the gaming experience of the future? With the rise of escape rooms, immersive theater, and virtual reality video games, the diversity of next generation game play options are rapidly multiplying and recombining to form a new genre of immersive experiences. This chapter considers the factors that gave rise to this reimagined form of entertainment. By exploring Two Bit Circus' Story Room and its show control system, Kyogen, this chapter considers the rise and possibilities of live-action adventure.

1 Sixty Minutes to Escape

Over the past 10 years, a new form of entertainment has broken into the mainstream. First gaining popularity in Asia and Europe, "Escape Rooms" offer an alternative way to spend an evening with friends. True to their name, the game play experience typically follows a similar outline: participants go to a physical location, willingly lock themselves in a room, and solve a series of puzzles in the hopes of escaping within the allotted 60 min. While the story veneer varies, the aim is constant: collect clues and solve puzzles to escape the room within the allotted time.

The experience begins with a group of individuals, usually between 6 and 12, who enter a room together and receive objectives to start their mission. Participants scour the room for clues, typically hidden in visual puzzles scattered about the space. Puzzles vary in style and content; typical escape rooms include a mix of visual clues, cryptography, missing or hidden elements, deductive reasoning, mazes, numeric codes, and sequencing challenges. The quality of production design varies since most escape rooms favor puzzles over immersion or story.

This genre of game-based entertainment has exploded with users readily embracing the experience as a novel alternative to movies or game nights. Escape rooms can be found from Hanoi to Des Moines with hundreds of different locations in cities across the world ("Escape Room Directory" 2015).

© The Author(s) 2015

E. Lemle et al., *Two Bit Circus and the Future of Entertainment*,
SpringerBriefs in Computer Science, DOI 10.1007/978-3-319-25793-8_3

2 Digital Puzzles

While the history of the escape room is largely self-generated by developers and enthusiasts, many users point to narrative and puzzle-based video games as the origin of the room escape game experience. A well-established game genre, first-person exploration-based games allow for greater immersion by providing "a vantage point that attempts to simulate looking through a game character's eyes" (First person perspective 2015). While there have been numerous popular first-person video games, the computer game *Myst* remains a defining title for gamers and escape room enthusiasts.

Originally released in 1993, *Myst* was one of the first CD-ROM games that utilized first-person exploration (Rosenberg 2013). The best selling computer game of the twentieth century, *Myst* ushered in a new level of quality for immersive puzzles. In the visually rich game, players explore an otherworldly island as they amass clues to solve challenging puzzles. As players are given little direction, much of game play includes casual exploration in a point-and-click world (Rosenberg 2013).

Thanks to advances in graphic technology, first-person puzzle-based games continue to enjoy popularity with contemporary gamers. Titles such as 2007s *Portal* emphasized puzzle solving embedded in a divergent narrative with compelling character development (Narcisse 2012).

The genre has also moved to mobile devices. 2013s *Device 6* is one such example (Sliva 2013). In the critically acclaimed title, players are guided through a richly puzzled and surreal soundscape that seems to break through the confines of the electronic device. The game is part adventure, part puzzle, part suspended disbelief, and part corporeal escape. Similar to *Myst*, the rich storyline and expertly embedded puzzle design combine to serve as a powerful experience for the player (Sliva 2013).

Most recently, such games have begun to transition to virtual reality platforms, allowing users to dive even deeper into immersive gaming experiences.

3 Theatrical Shifts

The emphasis on immersion continues to echo across entertainment genres; over the past 10 years, the landscape of contemporary American theatre has followed a similar trajectory.

Seeking a more immersive, participatory experience, American theatergoers are increasingly attending productions in abandoned car lots and in back rooms of bars. In these productions, seats are typically optional or absent. While the productions are diverse in nature and content, attendees are often encouraged to explore or interact beyond the typical separation provided by the proscenium stage. Productions are created around the opportunities and constraints provided by the physical spaces, resulting in theater, that when well executed, creates compelling immersion and fosters intimacy with the audience.

The Artistic Director of the Los Angeles-based immersive theater group the Wilderness, Annie Saunders, believes that "the impersonal nature of the digital era makes immersive theater particularly relevant for audiences" (Gelt 2015). Such an engagement allows for audience to have a visceral experience antithetical to the isolation of screen-based daily life.

Additionally, theatergoers are voting with their wallets in favor of productions that allow the enthusiast to participate in the experience. Touted by the La Jolla Playhouse as the "'next huge wave of growth in the American theater'" (Cox 2013), immersive theater experiences are popping up in cities from coast to coast.

Much of the recent success of the genre's expansion in the United States is thanks to the runaway success of *Sleep No More*, an immersive interpretation of Shakespeare's Macbeth. Developed by the London-based Punchdrunk, the current production of *Sleep No More* has been running in New York City since 2011 (Gelt 2015).

In the 3-h experience, participants are provided with masks and encouraged to explore the massive converted warehouse. Each of the 190 rooms are meticulously designed and accessorized, from the carefully lettered script in the leather-bound ledgers to the family portraits adorning peeling wallpaper. Participants are encouraged to explore, dig through the trash, sample abandoned candy, peek through keyholes, and indulge in voyeuristic imagination. Cast members wander throughout the space, occasionally pulling patrons into their individual storylines as they present their version of the classic tale. Rarely, however, is the visual content tied to character or plot development.

In his article "Immersive Theater and the Freedom of Choice, author Adam Green draws numerous parallels to the experience of *Sleep No More* and the rise of immersive theater to the popularity enjoyed by the adventure game *Myst* (2015). Green asserts that the "the whole 'Hey, what's over here' curiosity, eschewing typical forms of structured narration, stems not just from these expanded walls of gaming, but from the flattened world of the internet, which enables vast informational exploration, as well as highly-personalized experiences" (2015).

However, the comparison of immersive theater to video games is not without dissent, critics of *Sleep No More* have pointed out that despite the seeming autonomy of the immersive theater experience, in contrast to the first-person video game experience, none of the decisions made by the immersive theater attendee actually impact the experience. In his review of the experience, author Jason Schreier relates that the linear narrative of Sleep No More resulted in difficulty feeling "any sense of reward, or accomplishment, or even emotional gratification from your actions" (2011).

4 The Third Space

When considered in concert, these discrete cultural moments combine to create a compelling future for game play.

Two Bit Circus recognized an opportunity at the intersection of escape rooms, explorative video games, and immersive theater. The interdisciplinary organization saw an opportunity to leverage the power of modern computing and compelling narrative as bridges between entertainment genres, paring digital and physical elements for a live-action immersive game.

The result, Story Room, is an experience very much grounded in reality, but one where players are encouraged to suspend partial belief in the service of serious fun. Leveraging Two Bit Circus' technological and game-making expertise with professional theatrical chops, Story Room revolutionizes real-world immersive game play.

5 History

Avid supporters of the nascent escape room trend in Los Angeles, the Two Bit Circus team was interested in creating an experience that expanded the potential of escape rooms though technological integration and high-quality storytelling.

The project began in 2014 as a scribbled whiteboard of classic movie-inspired genres: the noir caper, the underwater accident, the sinister magician—no over-soaked theme discredited. Ultimately, the team decided on a well-worn trope of science fiction. Once the rough plot and theme were established, the team set to work creating a 16 by 16 foot room within the company headquarters.

During the 6-week development of the initial prototype and subsequent remount in spring of 2015, the team placed equal emphasis on creating engaging puzzles and developing compelling characters and plot. Puzzles that did not directly tie to the storyline were quickly eliminated or adapted to fit the constraints of the storyline. As a result, the user goal of Story Room is not to escape but to aid the fictional protagonist. In his review of the Story Room experience, author George Mandella concluded that the shift from escape to agency was "a subtle nuance, and therein lies all the difference" (2015). The beta test was a great success, receiving high marks from professional game makers and casual enthusiasts alike.

In *Story Room, Episode One: Cosmic Contagion,* players assumed the identity of "Team Beta", a team of investigators following up on the mysterious disappearance of a respected laboratory researcher. During game play, players activate clues and unlock puzzles through a series of individual components, each containing a Raspberry Pi microcomputer. Each of the discrete components connects to a network server. The components could be directly triggered through independent component interaction or remotely triggered through an operator's screen. As a result, players' decisions could result in multiple endings in *Cosmic Contagion* (Figs. 3.1 and 3.2).

The heart of the Story Room game play experience is Kyogen, a comprehensive proprietary show-control software system developed by Two Bit Circus Co-founder and CTO, Eric Gradman. Developed specifically for the Story Room platform, Kyogen provides an overarching software framework to control all production elements, storylines, and puzzles. Predominantly programmed in Python, Kyogen acts as a conductor for the overall experience; in addition to cueing lights, sound, and

Fig. 3.1 Still image from Two Bit Circus' Story Room Episode One: Cosmic Contagion. Image courtesy of Two Bit Circus

Fig. 3.2 Players search for hidden clues about the whereabouts of a missing scientist in Story Room Episode One: Cosmic Contagion. Image courtesy of Two Bit Circus

video and providing hints as needed, Kyogen unlocks evolving story points as players complete puzzle sequences. Kyogen is able to track the individual elements within Story Room, noting how individual components are configured and consequentially, how the players are progressing.

6 High-Tech Gameplay

The computer-driven experience provides a highly personalized gaming experience; similar to the "Choose Your Own Adventure" titles popularized in the 1980s and 1990s which are in part credited for the rise in narrative-driven video games (History of CYOA 2015), In Story Room, Kyogen allows for divergent and adaptive game play. Kyogen allows players to have agency, the choices Story Room participants impact subsequent story and puzzle development. Moreover, Kyogen is invisible to players, ensuring an immersive and multi-layered experience.

The computer program functions as the live-action storyteller, providing content and context as gameplay progresses. Additionally, Kyogen facilitates the human-to-human interaction core to the Two Bit Circus mission. The entire Story Room experience hinges on this symbiotic relationship; human teamwork, problem solving, and subsequent input are critical to story and puzzle advancement. Although the components can actuate automatically through Kyogen, human collaboration drives the story (Fig. 3.3).

Fig. 3.3 Members of the Two Bit Circus team prototyping a collaborative Story Room puzzle

The Kyogen framework allows Story Room to function almost autonomously, requiring very little of the operator. The operator only needs to run the initial program and the subsequent clusters will launch when appropriately triggered by the players.

Story Room and Kyogen also resolve a common challenge with escape rooms: broken immersion. At the conclusion of many existing room escape experiences, an operator enters the room and explains the puzzles, successes, and failures to the players. Not only does this break the immersion so carefully constructed over the previous hour, but also devalues the participants experience and relative success. In recent iterations, some room escape games have taken to giving players walkie-talkies to the same end. Kyogen by contrast adjusts the story to accommodate for the speed of the players, maintaining the immersion by providing hints where needed.

7 Moving Forward

After the 2014 prototype, there was consensus among the Story Room team that that the form and technology could be expanded and improved prior to a wider launch. Among other priorities, the team was interested in further developing Kyogen to provide for more adaptive game play and additional integration of hints and clues.

Building on the success and lessons of the first beta test, Two Bit Circus launched a second production of *Cosmic Contagion* in Spring 2015. Reimagined as a three-room experience, the revised version integrated additional puzzle components and more expansive gameplay options. Existing puzzles were expanded to complement the larger scale. For example, a small console-based navigation puzzle featured in the original production was reimagined for a full room. In the remounted version, up to six players take on simultaneous discrete tasks (driving the vehicle, powering the vehicle, deciphering maps, plotting the course, etc.) and must collaborate in order to complete the puzzle. Gradman further refined Kyogen, expanding the platform's back-end capability as well updating the graphical user interface to simplify the operator experience.

8 Conclusion

The combination of room escape games, first-person narrative video games, and immersive theater creates a compelling opportunity for defining avenues of play for the twenty-first century. As demonstrated through Story Room, connecting these discrete, yet complementary genres revolutionizes digital and physical play. Powered by advances in computer technology, Story Room transcends popular technology-based entertainment (Fig. 3.4).

Fig. 3.4 Signage from *Story Room Episode One: Cosmic Contagion*. Image courtesy of Two Bit Circus

References

Cox G (2013) Feeding the soul of stage: immersive theater mixes food, drink and environment staging to lure auds that eschew broadway. http://variety.com/2013/legit/news/feeding-the-soul-of-stage-1200413172/. Accessed 9 June 2015

Escape Room Directory (2015) http://escaperoomdirectory.com/. Accessed 9 June 2015

First person perspective (2015) http://www.giantbomb.com/first-person-perspective/3015-330/. Accessed 22 June 2015

Gelt J (2015) Immersive theater appeals to audiences wanting to take part in art. http://www.latimes.com/entertainment/arts/la-et-cm-day-shall-declare-it-20150305-story.html. Accessed 9 June 2015

Green A (2015) Immersive theater and the freedom of choice. http://www.tcgcircle.org/2013/04/immersive-theatre/. Accessed 9 June 2015

History of CYOA (2015). http://www.cyoa.com/pages/history-of-CYOA. Accessed 9 June 2015

Mandella G (2015) Saving the world is thirsty work. http://memelab.com/2015/05/26/story-room-saving-the-world-is-thirsty-work/. Accessed 9 June 2015

Narcisse E (2012) All-time 100 best video games: portal. http://techland.time.com/2012/11/15/all-time-100-video-games/slide/portal-2007/. Accessed 22 June 2015

Rosenberg A (2013) Myst co-creator looks back on his game's 20 year legacy. http://www.digitaltrends.com/gaming/myst-co-creator-robyn-miller-looks-back-on-his-games-20-year-legacy/. Accessed 8 June 2015

Schreier J (2011) Interactive play sleep no more feels like a game, but more confusing. http://www.wired.com/2011/08/sleep-no-more/. Accessed 9 June 2015

Sliva M (2013) The smartest game in the room. http://www.ign.com/articles/2013/11/27/device-6-review. Accessed 9 June 2015

Chapter 4
Virtual Reality and the Future of Entertainment

Abstract Virtual Reality (VR) is a form of immersive entertainment that is redefining traditional cinematic tools, practices, techniques, and narrative approaches. Two Bit Circus is leading innovation in this emerging genre of entertainment, creating VR content, inventing VR technology, and establishing new production processes in this 360°, 3D virtual reality space.

1 Prologue

To the uninitiated, someone experiencing virtual reality for the first time looks truly mad; a black box covering their eyes and strapped to their head, usually waving their hands around, running in place, and excitedly talking to people who do not exist.

The perceived madness resolves as soon as the skeptic pulls on the headset and finds himself instantly transported to a football stadium, standing inside of a stadium's tunnel, surrounded by his teammates. He runs out on to the field and takes his place on the line of scrimmage. He looks behind him, he is in a defensive position, preparing to receive a punt return from the opposing team. Craning his neck up to see the fans in the top seats in the stadium, he hears the roar of the crowd. Finally, the opposing team kicks the ball, it comes straight to him! He catches it, swiveling his head around to make sure his teammates are ready to block him as he starts charging towards the end zone. He runs into the end zone to complete the picture perfect touchdown. He's a hero! The crowd goes wild.

2 Definitions

Virtual reality (VR) is the digital production of an immersive and convincing audio-visual illusion, as defined by the New York Times (Heffernan 2014). Virtual reality headsets, or Head Mounted Displays (HMDs) are the vehicle for the VR experience; software seamlessly simulates a three-dimensional world that the user can manipulate and explore (Strickland 2007). Since the virtual world exists in 360°, the user feels truly immersed in the virtual setting from all angles of perception.

© The Author(s) 2015
E. Lemle et al., *Two Bit Circus and the Future of Entertainment*,
SpringerBriefs in Computer Science, DOI 10.1007/978-3-319-25793-8_4

Whether it is catching a football for a game winning touchdown, racing an IndyCar, or examining health care options with a medical provider, immersion is key to compelling virtual reality experiences. As the user becomes fully apart of the experience, immersion sets VR apart from other media platforms, specifically video games, which only go as far as first- person player views and captivating narratives.

3 Early Innovation

While the concepts and exploration of virtual reality can be traced back to the 1800s, it was the development of flight simulators for pilot training in the 1920s that initiated subsequent development of virtual reality as an immersive platform. Responsive and interactive, early flight simulators placed a pilot in an enclosed cockpit through use of a two-dimensional screen. The simulator would then tilt and move according to the feedback received from the pilot, creating an immersive experience for the participant (Rheingold 1991).

Patented in 1962, Mort Heilig's "Sensorama" (Fig. 4.1) is one of the first machines created to immerse the user into a sensory environment. To experience this gargantuan machine, the user sat in a seat and peered into an enclosed tunnel. The Sensorama showed a 3D film, along with stereo sound, aromas, and wind to create one of the first immersive environments aimed at the entertainment market (Turi 2014).

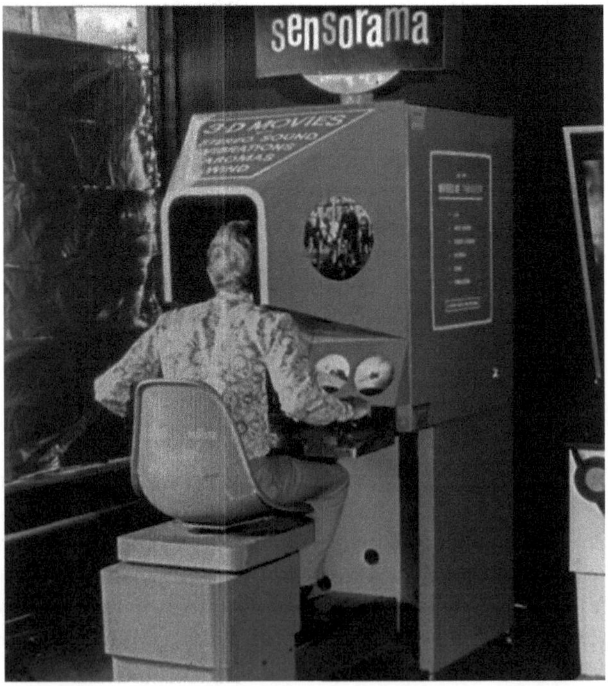

Fig. 4.1 Sensorama in use (Reproduced with permission from Marianne Heilig)

In 1968, Ivan Sutherland revealed a room-sized VR-like machine, supplemented by an enormous helmet so large, it had to be suspended by a mechanical support system within the room so it did not crush the wearer (Heffernan 2014).

Developments in graphic technology also spurred the development of VR. By the late 1970s, most of the special effects used in movies were computer-generated, leading to a boom in the video game industry (University of Illinois at Urbana-Champaign 2015). As computer graphics continued to develop and advance throughout the 1980s, the computer gaming industry began to become more mainstream, providing an important precursor to early VR work (University of Illinois at Urbana-Champaign 2015). Scientific visualization, or using computer graphics to transform numerical data into images, gave way to animation, which launched a new genre of entertainment.

High-performance computers, with powerful image rendering capabilities, allowed for humans and computers to interact in a more advanced way. Augmented reality, or a real world environment that is augmented by computer-generated input such as enhanced graphics, sounds, or location-related data, also emerged at this time (University of Illinois at Urbana-Champaign 2015).

Modern technology has allowed entertainment and gameplay to become consistently more immersive, allowing for enhanced viewing and playing experiences. Flight simulators, early VR experiences, and the advancement of computer technology and computer graphics have all paved the way for VR to become a new immersive platform.

4 Current Platforms

Head-mounted displays (HMDs) are the most common platform for viewing VR content. Although HMDs were first developed in the 1960s (Rheingold 1991), the hardware has become increasingly popular in recent years, most notably due to Facebook's purchase of virtual reality company Oculus for $2 billion dollars in early 2015 (Heffernan 2014; Fig. 4.2).

Oculus burst onto the scene in 2012 with a successfully funded $2+ million Kickstarter campaign. In their campaign, Oculus pitched the "Rift" HMD, a VR product for the individual consumer (Benedictus 2014). Since the initial campaign, the Rift has gone through various iterations, most of which have been sold to the public as "development kits" to give developers time to create content for the product's full release (Warren 2013). The Rift uses custom displays and advanced optics specifically designed for VR to create high resolution visual clarity (Oculus 2015). The headset has 360° orientation and advanced position tracking. Integrated headphones and an audio system customized for VR compatibility set the sound stage for the VR experience (Oculus 2015).

Currently, PC-based model like the Rift have the most advanced capabilities, including tracking head and body movements to simulate full-body immersion while in use (Super Data Research 2015). Light mobile devices, such as Google's

Fig. 4.2 Oculus Rift

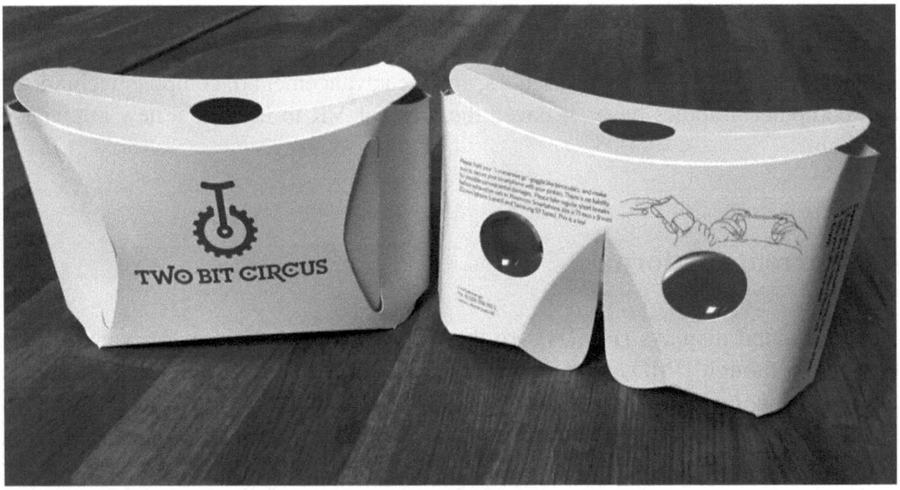

Fig. 4.3 Two Bit Circus VR viewer from i-mmersive

do-it-yourself version of VR called Google Cardboard, are smartphone attachments that render a rudimentary VR experience. Premium mobile devices like the Samsung Gear VR (Fig. 4.4) use smartphones as the base screen but have advanced software for features such as position tracking. Console devices like Sony's Morpheus, currently under development, will have similar capabilities to the PC-based models (Super Data Research 2015). Similar to the Cardboard VR product, German company i-mmersive has created a paper VR viewer and released two mobile-compatible VR apps (Fig. 4.3).

Other notable platforms include Vive (an acronym for Very Immersive Visual Experience) by HTC and Valve, promising a full room-scale experience (Savov 2015).

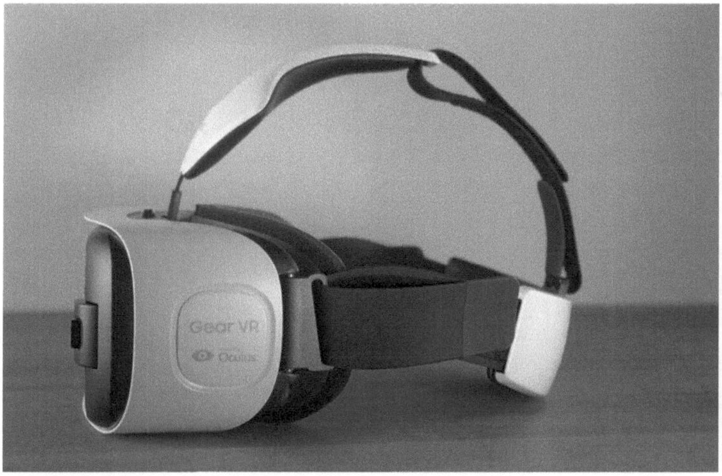

Fig. 4.4 Samsung Gear VR

Using a laser-based motion tracking system, Vive knows where the user's head at all times, data that the Valve's software interprets to generate a highly accurate picture of what the user is doing in a three-dimensional space. Another virtual reality platform, Leap Motion, allows the player to use their bare hands as controllers, without bulky gloves or handheld devices, that allows the player to switch between augmented and virtual reality worlds (Leap Motion 2015).

Microsoft's much anticipated HoloLens is a fully untethered, see-through holographic computer that enables holographic images to integrate into physical spaces for an experience Microsoft calls "mixed reality" (Microsoft 2015). While the HoloLens is expected to have multiple applications, avid gamers are anticipating a commercial release as the product allows players to use any physical surface as a gaming portal, to control the game using voice commands, and to integrate existing physical objects in the space into the game (Microsoft 2015).

There has been incredible interest in HMDs for delivery of VR experiences. Developers continue to improve common issues associated with HMDs. However, current challenges such as latency with display performance, limited field of view, integrated interaction technology, and heavily wired devices for viewing more comprehensive content continue to limit hardware adoption (Baker A., Personal Conversation 2015).

4.1 The Three-Dimensional Puzzle

Two Bit Circus recognizes the tremendous opportunity that VR presents. With Chief Content Officer Nancy Bennett at the helm, the company's virtual reality team is leading the industry in respects to live-action VR filming; servicing clients such as

Fig. 4.5 Two Bit Circus Chief Content Officer Nancy Bennett. Image courtesy of Two Bit Circus

Verizon, the NFL, the NBA, Samsung, and the United States Olympic Committee. Bennett and her team are defining the industry by creating original content, inventing new filming technologies, and establishing best practices for production in the virtual reality space.

"Imagine solving a crossword puzzle in 3-D," says Bennett. "That's what it's like to produce virtual reality content," she relates, revealing a sphinx-like smile. "It's like solving a *spherical*, crossword puzzle" (Personal Conversation 2015; Fig. 4.5).

Creating a puzzle poses even more challenges than creating it, and Bennett is doing both simultaneously: developing the content and the tools for immersive virtual reality experiences. With over 30 years worth of experience in entertainment, Bennett drives the creative vision with her team—Jay Spanglar, Spencer Hochberg, and Aaron Thomen. Breaking traditional filmmaking rules, the Two Bit Circus VR team is forging new tools and techniques for a 360°, 3D canvas.

4.2 *Creative Decision-Making: Technology and Content*

Given the diversity of possible applications and directions for VR, content creators must make a series of key decisions, beginning with the decision between live-action versus computer-generated images (CGI). Two Bit Circus chose to specialize in live-action VR experiences; recent VR work explores the perspective of professional athletes. Engineer Hochberg asserts that with live-action sports VR, the participant gains otherwise unattainable insight into the lives and training of professional athletes, stating that with live-action VR, the participant is "on their adventure" (Personal Conversation 2015). The possibilities within the subgenre provide experiential questions for Bennett and team to answer: "What does a basketball player see on the court? What does an NFL punt return look like? What's it like to be with all those football players in the tunnel? What's it like to sit in an IndyCar and go 70 miles per hour?" (Personal Conversation 2015).

Engineer Aaron Thomen further supports the current focus, asserting that "first-person, immersive experiences are best for VR... anything that is awe-inspiring, adrenaline boosting, or anything that someone wouldn't be able to experience on their own. Most people won't go explore on a submarine, or go out in space, or run down a football field for a touchdown", yet with VR, viewers can participate in such unusual experiences (Personal Conversation 2015). Virtual reality provides compelling alternatives for those who are not destined to be professional athletes, racecar drivers, or adrenaline junkies.

4.3 Mediums and Narrative Opportunities

Trailblazing Bennett and her team experiment with groundbreaking storytelling techniques in a space with new and constantly evolving rules. Bennett asserts that "immersion is the new engagement....the challenge of VR is directing the viewer's eye and ear" (Personal Conversation 2015). As participants drive the action, VR creators face the challenge of utilizing the full space while encouraging the viewer to participate and interact with the visual content. Virtual reality is unique among media platforms as the viewer's role changes and the viewer is an active participant.

Additionally, as the VR viewer behaves autonomously, creators must cue the viewer visually or aurally to guide them through the experience. Bennett stresses the importance of this cuing stating that equally important are "the hints of story, plot, emotion, and/or psychological development...[and how] to always advance the story and develop character." Bottom line is, "If you're not doing either, you're not doing a good job" (Personal Conversation 2015).

4.4 VR Innovation @ Two Bit Circus

Two Bit Circus' innovative approach to VR has led the team to create groundbreaking content. Before beginning a project, the Two Bit Circus team gives careful consideration to the creative goal of each opportunity, considering how VR-specific media will elevate narrative content. Moreover, when pitching a project to a prospective client, the Two Bit Circus team takes time to craft carefully considered pitches and film treatments that evoke powerful and emotional storytelling. This emphasis on storytelling and immersion, core to the content Two Bit Circus creates, has led to exciting projects for Bennett and team.

In 2014, Wasserman and Verizon Indycar contracted the Two Bit Circus team to create a VR motion platform using Oculus Rift. Tasked with the challenge of recreating the heart-pulsing action of travelling 170 miles per hour, the Two Bit Circus team first needed to solve how effectively capture multiple perspectives from a vehicle travelling at top speed.

To solve this quandary, the team began by prototyping custom 3D printed GoPro enclosures (Fig. 4.6).

The enclosure contained 16 cameras arranged to capture 360° of action. The team then installed the camera rig in the body of the Verizon Indycar (Fig. 4.7).

A professional driver drove the Indycar at top speed around the Long Beach, California racetrack, simultaneously capturing footage from all 16 cameras. With filming complete, the Two Bit Circus team created custom software to stitch the individual camera feeds together. The final footage was piped into an Oculus Rift HMD.

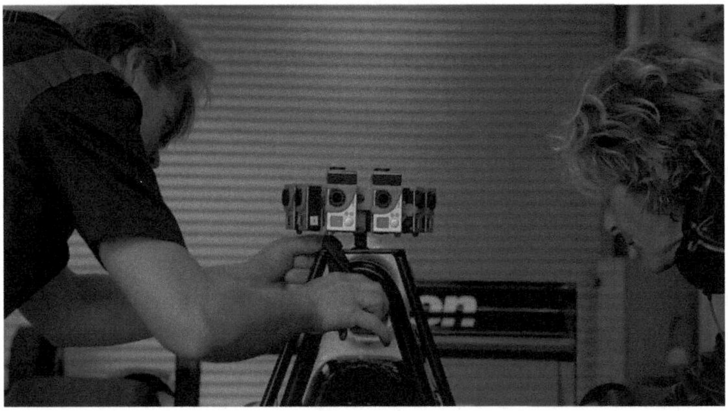

Fig. 4.6 Members of the Two Bit Circus VR team adjusting a prototype GoPro enclosure

Fig. 4.7 Two Bit Circus GoPro Rig attached to Verizon Indycar for filming

Fig. 4.8 Replica Verizon Indycar motion tracking platform

Concurrently, the team built a custom motion simulation platform to fully recreate the driving experience. A full-scale replica of the Verizon Indycar, the platform tracked movement of the racecar to articulated movements of the replica chair, resulting in a fully immersive user experience (Fig. 4.8).

The team followed a similar process for a subsequent project with Wasserman and Verizon for an VR experience for fans at Superbowl XXLV (Figs. 4.9 and 4.10).

For this project, the team recreated the experience of catching a punt return and running to the endzone for a touchdown. Again the content featured a powerful emotional narrative amplified by a 360°, 3D first-person perspective (Fig. 4.11).

To capture the first-person experience at eye-level, the Two Bit Circus team experimented with several types of camera rigs, including mounting the GoPro enclosure to the top of football helmet, prior to settling on a modified electric tricycle.

The Two Bit Circus team continues to be a leader in capturing the powerful stories of professional athletes; other recent projects include creating content for Samsung Milk VR with NBA All-Stars as well as Olympic athletes as part of the road to the 2016 Rio de Janeiro Olympics. The team continues to find innovative ways of capturing the 360°, 3D experience for maximum emotional parity; to fully capture the emotional thrill of Olympic pole vaulting, engineer (and professional unicyclist) Hochberg unicycled alongside the Olympian, the 360-camera rig strapped to his head (Personal Conversation 2015).

Fig. 4.9 Two Bit Circus Concept Image for NFL fan experience

Fig. 4.10 Team member Jay Spanglar adjusting the helmet height in the actualized product

Fig. 4.11 Screenshot from Game Time Experience

4.5 Facing New Challenges

Given their work in unchartered territory, the team's successes have not been without challenges. Bennett explains that while the most challenging aspects of contemporary VR production include addressing how to effectively capture the story in "360° without the filming team being anywhere near the camera and for many, without seeing what the camera sees", post-production remains the toughest obstacle (Personal Conversation 2015). To create compelling content, the VR director must skillfully address "multiple captures…multiple eyeballs…cameras—and stitch [individual camera feeds] together without seams" (Personal Conversation 2015). This presents a challenge not only in figuring out how and what to film, but in post-production as well.

As a result, VR content providers, including Two Bit Circus, must develop proprietary methods for combining individual film perspectives which, when combined or "stitched" together, result in the 360° perspective.

Two Bit Circus' VR production team is also limited by the current editing and stitching software. Existing software assumes distance between the VR viewer and film subject, a problem for first-person perspective. As a result, Engineer Thomen has been building and improving the editing software to improve the user experience. Prior to building the software, Thomen considered potential obstacles, recalling: "imagining how things would work in my mind. [considering] how [the geometries] worked…[before] trying to match what I'm seeing in my mind to what's programmed" (Personal Conversation 2015). The combination of existing and proprietary software has allowed the team to prototype, revise, and innovate quickly.

Hochberg compares the challenges of VR creation to "attempting to take water out of the ocean…[with] no limit to how many times you go there with your bucket" (Personal Conversation 2015). As the team strives for perfection, high-quality standards result in constant desire for improvement. As a result, the team refines their process with each VR project, subsequently improving production and post-production techniques. Despite current challenges, Bennett and team remain committed to the iterative process: "It's trial and error, and it's improving every time" (Personal conversation 2015).

5 Conclusion: Envisioning the Future

Virtual reality has powerful implications for the future of multiple industries, with innovators across entertainment, healthcare, education, and business applying evolving technology to solve current problems. While challenges remain, innovators like Bennett and the Two Bit Circus team continue to iterate, elevating the form and content standards.

The team's success stems from their interdisciplinary backgrounds, their creative approach to problem solving, and more importantly, their adventurous mindset. Bennett compares the VR production process to pioneering: "When you venture, there's discovery, thrill and knowledge. Implementing creative is important for the path of discovery. [Working in VR is] very much like discovering the Wild West, or flying to Mars. We don't know the outcome, but we learn so much, which answers other questions along the way" (Personal conversation 2015).

References

Benedictus L (2014) Why oculus's $2bn sale to facebook sparks fury from kickstarter funders.http://www.theguardian.com/technology/shortcuts/2014/mar/26/oculus-rift-facebook-fury-kickstarter-funders. Accessed 29 June 2015

Heffernan V (2014) Virtual reality fails its way to success. http://www.nytimes.com/2014/11/16/magazine/virtual-reality-fails-its-way-to-success.html. Accessed 26 June 2015

Leap Motion (2015) Leap motion for virtual reality. https://www.leapmotion.com/product/vr. Accessed 29 June 2015

Microsoft HoloLens (2015) Home. https://www.microsoft.com/microsoft-hololens/en-us. Accessed 29 June 2015

Oculus VR (2015) The oculus rift, oculus touch, and vr games at e3. https://www.oculus.com/en-us/blog/the-oculus-rift-oculus-touch-and-vr-games-at-e3/. Accessed 29 June 2015

Rheingold H (1991) Virtual reality. https://www.nsa.gov/public_info/_files/cryptologic_quarterly/Virtual_Reality.pdf. Accessed 23 June 2015

Savov V (2015) I wore the vive VR headset and didn't want to take it off. http://www.theverge.com/2015/3/4/8146523/htc-vive-valve-vr-headset-hands-on-preview. Accessed 29 June 2015

Strickland J (2007) How virtual reality works. http://electronics.howstuffworks.com/gadgets/other-gadgets/virtual-reality.htm. Accessed 25 June 2015

Super Data Research (2015) Virtual reality market brief 2015. www.superdataresearch.com. Accessed 25 June 2015

Turi J (2014) The sights and scents of the sensorama simulator. http://www.engadget.com/2014/02/16/morton-heiligs-sensorama-simulator/. Accessed 28 June 2015

University of Illinois at Urbana-Champaign (2015) Virtual reality: history. http://archive.ncsa.illinois.edu/Cyberia/VETopLevels/VR.History.html. Accessed 29 June 2015

Warren T (2013) Josh, the oculus rift, and a codpiece on late night with jimmy fallon. http://www.theverge.com/2013/1/31/3936288/josh-late-night-jimmy-fallon-oculus-rift-razer-edge-blackberry-z10-video. Accessed 29 June 2015

Chapter 5
Interview with Brent N. Bushnell, Co-Founder and CEO of Two Bit Circus

Abstract The chapter is taken from interviews conducted with Two Bit Circus Co-Founder and CEO, Brent Bushnell by Two Bit Circus Learning Engineer, Katherine Bomkamp. In the interview, Bushnell recounts his early inspiration as an inventor and entrepreneur, the founding of Two Bit Circus, current opportunities in computer science, and the rewards and challenges of entrepreneurship.

1 Interview with Brent N. Bushnell

Katherine Bomkamp: When did you know that you were first an inventor?

Brent Bushnell: I would say [in high school] when my brother and I made our collectible tradable card game... We loved Magic: The Gathering and so we'd made our own version that was like a sci-fi space version.

Katherine Bomkamp: Was that the first thing that you've ever invented?

Brent Bushnell: No. My brother and I loved making our own video games, we designed our own game console and we designed our own levels...[but]I oftentimes think of inventions as being physical stuff...One of my favorite high school professors and my Physics professor had us come up with an invention: we had to do a patent search, we had to really make a prototype....one of them was a stair-safe baby walker. [In our version of the solution] ... the second the baby walker would fall off a stair, the wheels would collapse and it would rest on bumpers so the baby couldn't move around... The other [design challenge] was a solution that would wake up drivers who are falling asleep at the wheel... Those were pretty real inventions where we did patent searches, made prototypes, that was really fun.

Katherine Bomkamp: How did you move from these experiences of knowing and then like understanding that you are an inventor to actually deciding to start a company? What were the skills what were the steps along the way?

© The Author(s) 2015

E. Lemle et al., *Two Bit Circus and the Future of Entertainment*,
SpringerBriefs in Computer Science, DOI 10.1007/978-3-319-25793-8_5

Brent Bushnell: So, my dad is a nerd—he's formally trained as an engineer, but always was [an] entrepreneur. And he really raised us with both those [attributes] ...Sundays with Dad was ramen, you know, eating ramen and going to Price Electronics and really tinkering with projects....[We] hijacked all the old phone lines in our house to install an Ethernet network... doing those kinds of things, but then he was also pushing us into doing entrepreneurial stuff.

I was a terrible baseball player but sold candy bars for my baseball team and sold magazine subscription sales to raise money for the school and my brother and I made jewelry and they sold that out in front of parking [lots and]... we took mistletoe and wrapped it in red ribbons and sold that out in front of the supermarket. So all year round we were selling [and] trying to sell things.

I always knew that I was going to be some blend of engineer and entrepreneur.

The very first company my brother and I started was outsource IT business right around 2000. We would do web hosting, web design, e-mail hosting. We helped small businesses [become] technical. This was before Gmail and so a lot of [the necessary skills and technology, running one's own servers] was hard...That [experience] was really the first step [in] doing my own business development, running the whole company, having bank accounts...

Katherine Bomkamp: And then, what brought you and [Two Bit Circus Co-Founder Eric Gradman] together (Fig. 5.1)?

Fig. 5.1 Bushnell (*left*) with father Nolan Bushnell (*center*) and Co-Founder Eric Gradman (*right*). Image courtesy of Two Bit Circus

Brent Bushnell: Eric and I met in 2007. We were all … invited by [our mutual friend] Doug Campbell to Barbara's Bar basically to share projects we were working on… sort of a nerd meet-up drinking club. And, the night Eric and I met … after the meet up was over, we went back to his place and we just started building our first project together which is this thing we called Art Fall (Fig. 5.2) which is this interactive white board. And [we created our first invention] the day we met and we've been building stuff together ever since.

Katherine Bomkamp: When did you know that you were on to something?

Brent Bushnell: We took [Art Fall] to a party and people liked it. And so, we kept making more stuff and taking [the projects to] more parties. The first time we got paid to do that was really special. [Our first paid event was for] Microsoft, we did their E3 party and we were the entertainment… And so, the margins [for events] were awesome, it's really like wow, this is pretty neat…that was a watershed moment. When we ended up on Extreme Makeover and [were part of a team that made a viral video for Los Angeles-based rock band] OK Go… we were getting a little bit of a reputation and all of a sudden we started to

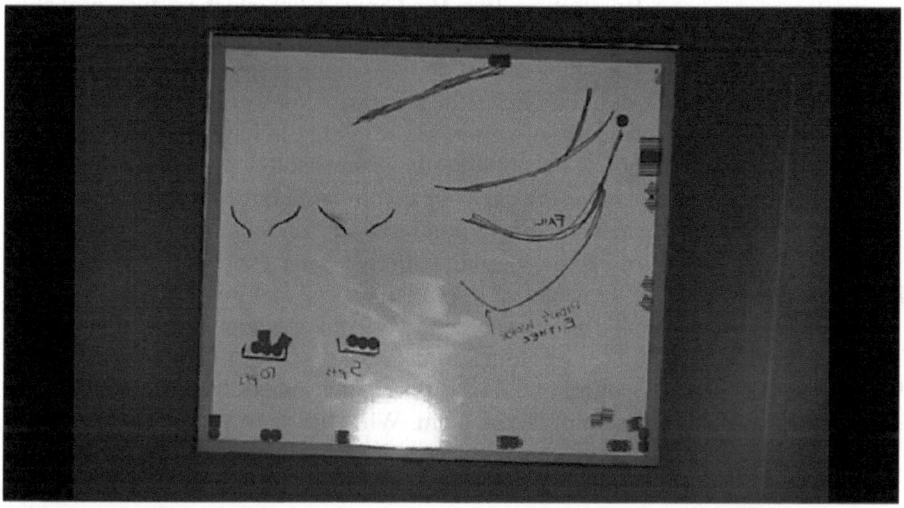

Fig. 5.2 A screen capture from Art Fall, Bushnell and Gradman's first joint project. This interactive art piece uses a standard white board, camera, and projector. In the experience, users draw on the white board, the shapes are picked up by the camera, and the resulting position translated through a computer program. The computer program in turn models and projects a physics model on to the white board, resulting in real-time dynamic physical and digital manipulation. Image courtesy of Two Bit Circus

[have many doors open]. And that was an early indicator of like, wow, we're doing something special even though we're not making a ton of money at it, we are doing stuff that is affecting people.

For Two Bit [Circus] the big transition moment was when our team swelled to like thirty doing a lot of our early projects …[and] had raised the money [to launch STEAM Carnival on crowd-funding platform] Kickstarter and really had some of our own [intellectual property]—that was another big moment of like, hey, this is the real thing!

Katherine Bomkamp: [From] everything I know about you and about your family, [it seems as if for you, entrepreneurship] is not that scary and [you grew] up in that culture where it was okay to go out and do those things, but making that leap to starting a company where there is nothing else out there like it—What is that experience like?

Brent Bushnell: When people get scared about entrepreneurship they're worried about not having the money that they are going to need to pay for their lifestyle and their reality. I've never really had designs on a nice car and what not, and so, on one side it reduced some of that risks and fear, on the other side [I] always felt kind of unemployable so there was sort of no other option. [Laughs]

[In starting Two Bit Circus,] I think there was probably increased comfort with the unpredictability of entrepreneurships since I've been doing it for so long—[for example] you don't really know… are we going to get that big contract or …not, are we going to have that success or … not. [I became] pretty comfortable with that early,… once you've maxed your credit cards out like three times, and then are able to pull it off and get them paid down, you get more comfortable with that crazy exposure.

Katherine Bomkamp: The nature of doing interesting and innovative things usually brings people to you, but… who is the ideal person to …realize your vision?

Brent Bushnell: I think one of the things that makes Two Bit [Circus] so amazing is the team. What has been so special about this group is people have a real diversity of skill set… we have a lot of folks that are multi-disciplinary. One of the questions that I have always asked [when hiring individuals] for all of our companies …is what do you do on the weekends? What that reveals is not only … what people are good at and what you're hiring them for, but also, … [an] indicator of what do [they] love, what keeps [them] going, what are [they] excited about.

And that has been a really important one for us because we're looking for folks that are passionate…and if they're really passionate about snails, chances are that they have the capacity to get excited about other stuff. But if they're not excited about anything, then it's hard press that they're going to be excited about what they're doing with us.

It has been a really good indicator to find folks who have crazy passions … and [do] lots of [different and unusual] things. We have always looked for folks with that sort of diversity.

Katherine Bomkamp: How is your background as an entrepreneur and an engineer informed your leadership?

Brent Bushnell: I think it's really important for an entrepreneur and a leader to be able to connect with people on a broad spectrum of levels. You think about a functioning company and it's got an accounting group and it's got a marketing group and it's got an engineering group and so for me working as an entrepreneur and having in the early phases of a company you wear all the hats. You're accounting, you're marketing, you're doing all of it…

And so, you run up against a lot of those challenges and hopefully as you grow a company; you find people that are better than you with each of those domains and you take off that hat and you give it to them. [For example] I'm taking off the accounting hat and I'm giving it to an accounting person who can now [assume those responsibilities]; but at least I can speak with them on a level of some understanding of what it is that they're doing and the challenges they're having. Being able to at least not be completely in the dark about it helps to be able to talk with that person and explore what's next; chances are I've had at least some understanding of what it is that's going on. I think that's really critical.

We are a very technical company, so my background as an engineer is helpful in talking with clients. I roughly know what I can sell, I might not be the one writing the code anymore or manufacturing it, but I know at least the state of the industry and can go out and look at other people's solutions and see what technical advancements they're incorporating. [This is important when] talking to the client, hav[ing] a rough idea of what it is that I can sell and what it's going to cost to do it…

Katherine Bomkamp: What excites you the most about computer science and the future of computer science?

Brent Bushnell: We are at this perfect storm right now where the [computer science] tools are getting super easy. My favorite example is the Hello World example: You know programming thirty years ago, the fundamental introduction, is how do you get Hello World (Fig. 5.3).
In Assembly Language that's punishing and terrible, right? You know it's twenty lines a code and it's foreign – it's Greek (Figs. 5.4).
[Today] in Python, [writing "Hello World" is] one line code (Fig. 5.5) and in [visual programming language,] Scratch, it's pictures on your iPad. And so, the tools are finally easy enough that it's not just for computer science graduates

```
      .MODEL  TINY
      .CODE
CODE    SEGMENT BYTE PUBLIC 'CODE'
      ASSUME  CS:CODE,DS:CODE
      ORG     0100H
      DB  'HELLO WORLD$', 0
      INC DH
      MOV AH,9
      INT 21H
      RET
```

ca 1980

Fig. 5.3 Programming "Hello World" example circa 1980. Image courtesy of Two Bit Circus

```
#include<stdio.h>

main()
{
   printf("Hello World");

}
```

ca 1990

Fig. 5.4 An example of "Hello World" from 1990 Bushnell uses as an example of a "slightly less terrible" example of accessible programming (Personal Conversation 2015). Image courtesy of Two Bit Circus

```
print "Hello World"
```

ca 2000

Fig. 5.5 An example from the 2000s, where programming syntax more closely mirrors natural language

[and] PhDs, but there really can be the tools within anybody's hands, most specifically the artists and the creatives. So now, all of a sudden, the set of tools that are available to the creatives are now much more powerful. I'm really excited to see like what's the current batch of graduates from the theater department are going to do now that they have access to micro controllers and cloud services.

Katherine Bomkamp: That's awesome. What about a current project most excites you?

Brent Bushnell: Two Bit [Circus] is now on the road of building out the productions that I see as our next decade of work. We will have our own traveling carnival. We are close to having our own installed story rooms, these are two steps on the way to having our own traveling interactive show, our own immersive theater… Over the next decade, [there will be] time for us to have a whole suite of different kinds of interactive, out-of-home entertainment—and the fact that it's working and people are excited about [Two Bit Circus' work] is really thrilling.

Katherine Bomkamp: If you have a time machine, what would you invent or create in the future? Or you're already doing it?

Brent Bushnell: Yeah, man, I mean we're building exactly what I want to have in the future. [Laughs] So, yeah, I would say we're actively building that out… I want to re-imagine … whole swaths of out-of-home entertainment and capitalize on underutilized assets, make restaurants compelling on Sunday and Monday night, made stadiums awesome when there's no football game, turn band and hockey rinks into something cool when it's not hockey season, really turn all of those places into fun interactive experiences with augmented by technology [and] made possible by technology.

Katherine Bomkamp: One of your favorite quotes [from author Madeleine L'Engle] that is [that] inspiration comes during work, rather than before it. What does that mean in the context of Two Bit [Circus and] in the context of your personal work?

Brent Bushnell: At Two Bit [Circus] we're rapid prototypers, Eric and I always laugh that oftentimes the things we're the most excited about end up being the dumbest. [Laughs] And that's really important, right? Because if we're just sitting on the couch and coming up with ideas, we're in an echo chamber—Yeah, we've never met an idea we didn't like of our own, you know?!

But Madeleine L'Engle's quote… Inspiration comes during work—it's only when you actually get down to brass tacks and start building it and testing it that you start to realize what sucks and what's awesome.

And so, because technology is this wonderful space and we can do a good job of prototyping things quickly…[we are in] a really powerful position to be able to figure out what's good quickly by this afternoon or by this weekend…To come up with an idea and then sit down and actually build it and then be like, okay, is this awesome or not… and now let's make version two. [Thanks to modern technology,] that whole process can take a day… and ten years ago would have taken you a year, that sort of quick rapid iteration is so powerful.

I think that [the ability to rapidly prototype] is an asset for Two Bit [Circus], it's something that is really powerful—My dad was always hammering into us is when were kids—he would say, "I don't care if the company you're talking about is going to make a million dollars in a year—How can you make one dollar this weekend?"

And that was really powerful because the entrepreneur is a doer, not a thinker, and you get so much feedback by going out and testing things. Chances are your idea is bad and wrong, but once you get out there and start testing it, you start to realize, wow, this is what's wrong about it, let me change that thing and now it becomes good, great even.

Katherine Bomkamp: What is the most frustrating thing that you've come up against either in the industry or as an entrepreneur?

Brent Bushnell: One of the most frustrating things about being a small business [and] being a startup is dealing with the long time it takes to interact with big corporations. [Since large corporations tend to move more slowly]…your sale cycle takes three months, six months, twelve months, once you finally get them to agree to the work, the contract negotiation takes another few months.

Now, you're finally able to do the work, the thing that you love, right? You're finally able to execute on the work and now it's time for them to pay you. Depending on who they are, your payment terms, [you will receive payment] thirty days, most likely they're sixty days or most in the worst case they're a hundred and twenty days [after completion of the work]. A hundred and twenty days, a third of the year, they're going to pay you a third of the year after you do the work? I mean that is crushing.

And so, for a small business it is—that is really running really hand to mouth, those time frames can be meaningful and incapacitating…It underscores [that] it's not enough to

	just do the work, you really need to have a whole infrastructure around you to make sure that you can withstand those long time tables.
Katherine Bomkamp:	What is the most surprising thing?
Brent Bushnell:	The most surprising thing is how is this magic fairy dust that is on this company right now…I've [started] a lot of different companies and a lot of time it feels like you're pushing so hard uphill—[pitching to potential clients like: "]hey, you want this, please you want this, really you want this["… you are] trying to convince everybody. [At Two Bit Circus] it's been the opposite, it just has a natural momentum, people reach out and they want to be involved—whether it's partners, or customers, or sponsors, or media, or employees, or what not it has a magic to it that frankly is magic because I don't actually have a clear formula for how I would recreate it, and that's really weird because we've been here the whole time doing it, but yet there was some special combination and swirling set of conditions that got [Two Bit Circus] that magic…[that magic is] hard to recreate.
Katherine Bomkamp:	It's pretty awesome.
Brent Bushnell:	It's pretty awesome.
Katherine Bomkamp:	Do you have anything else you want to add?
Brent Bushnell:	I don't think so. That's great.
Katherine Bomkamp:	Cool.
Brent Bushnell:	Awesome.

MIX
Papier aus verantwortungsvollen Quellen
Paper from responsible sources
FSC® C105338

If you have any concerns about our products,
you can contact us on
ProductSafety@springernature.com

In case Publisher is established outside the EU,
the EU authorized representative is:
Springer Nature Customer Service Center GmbH
Europaplatz 3, 69115 Heidelberg, Germany

Printed by Libri Plureos GmbH
in Hamburg, Germany